The Formac Pocketguide to

Nova Scotia
Birds

80 Seashore & Water Birds

Written & illustrated by Jeffrey C. Domm

Formac Publishing Company Limited
Halifax, Nova Scotia

Formac Publishing Company Limited acknowledges the support of the Cultural Affairs Section, Nova Scotia Department of Tourism and Culture. We acknowledge the financial support of the Government of Canada through the Book Publishing Industry Development Program (BPIDP) for our publishing activities. We acknowledge the support of the Canada Council for the Arts for our publishing program.

National Library of Canada Cataloguing in Publication Data

Domm, Jeff, 1958-
    The Formac pocketguide to Nova Scotia birds

(Formac pocketguide)
Includes index.
Contents: [v. 1] 120 common inland birds – v. 2. 80 seashore and water birds
ISBN 0-88780-507-8 (v. 1).—ISBN 0-88780-515-9 (v. 2)

    1. Birds—Nova Scotia—Identification. 2. Bird watching—Nova Scotia—Guidebooks. I. Title. II. Series.

QL685.5.N6D65 2000   598'.09716   C00-950155-X

Cartography by Peggy McCalla

Formac Publishing Company Limited
5502 Atlantic Street
Halifax, Nova Scotia
Canada B3H 1G4

Printed and bound in Canada

Contents

Introduction

Situated on the migration path of the Atlantic flyway, Nova Scotia is an excellent place to observe birds which breed in northern Canada and travel to temperate southern climates in winter. Some of these migrants, such as ducks, make their winter home around the Nova Scotia coast, while others continue their flight south.

This makes Nova Scotia is an ideal area for observing birds, especially water and shore birds. The lakes and rivers, and the variety of coastal landscapes are habitats for numerous species. Along the Atlantic coast, in the sheltered bays and on uninhabited islands, many coastal and off-shore birds can be seen. The towering cliffs on the north-east coast of Cape Breton Island are nesting grounds for guillemots, kittiwakes and many species of gulls, including the Iceland Gull. Bird Island, off this same shore, is the breeding ground for some sea birds that are never seen on the mainland, including the Atlantic Puffin. Along the northwest shore of the mainland, the sand beaches and adjacent marshes are feeding areas for resident and migrant birds. The tidal phenomenon of the Bay of Fundy creates a unique landscape of steep cliffs, stone beaches and vast areas of mudflats where bird life is abundant. At the western end of the bay is Brier Island where many migrating birds, as well as numerous species of resident sea birds, can be seen. The Yarmouth area, at the southern tip of the province, is an area of special interest to birders because of some unusual species that can be seen in freshwater locations and on offshore islands. The Birding Hot Spots listed on pages 8-15 give some suggestions of places to start birding.

When observing birds in the wild it isn't always easy to make a correct identification, especially if the birds are a great distance away. The visual keys in this book will help you quickly compare what you see with a bird depicted here. The full-colour illustrations, painted especially for this book, are drawn from several sources, including photographs, observations, scientific specimens and written descriptions. They emphasize the key features — shape, colour, markings and size. Each one represents a typical specimen: it is helpful to remember that plumage variations are to be expected and that colours change in different light conditions. In addition, many birds change plumage seasonally and this book gives the coloration most likely to be seen in Nova Scotia.

Along with each full-colour illustration, there are diagrams that depict the seasonal range, the size, the type of foot, the rhythm of the flight pattern, a characteristic way of feeding, and for those birds that breed in Nova Scotia a colour rendition of an egg.

This guide, Volume 2 of the Formac Pocket Guide to Nova Scotia Birds, introduces 80 water and shore birds most likely to be seen in Nova Scotia. (Volume 1 presented 120 inland birds.) Many of them are birds you can expect to see anywhere in the region; others have more limited range and are found in specific areas.

The contents are arranged in alphabetical order of genus names which are found on the top of each page. The species are arranged alphabetically in each genus group.

Before setting out on a birdwatching trip in Nova Scotia, be sure to dress warmly and watch the weather. Storms can move in quickly over the ocean and bring high winds and cold temperatures, even in summer. These changes can affect the number of birds you see, not to mention dampening your spirits.

Nova Scotia is fortunate in still having areas of forest and coastline that are almost completely isolated from human activity. However, the threat of human contact is increasing daily. Only two percent of Nova Scotia beaches are formally restricted from development; industrial waste is evident in water and on land; and the protection of species is far behind that of other countries. One species, the Piping Plover, has received some attention with the Piping Plover Guardian Program. Signs have been posted to mark nesting locations and volunteers watch over the nests and conduct public education sessions in an effort to preserve the species from disturbance.

Birds of all sizes play an important role in the balance of nature. Their place in the food chain has been severely disrupted by desertification, deforestation and by the widespread use of pesticides in agriculture. With this guide you can readily appreciate the abundant variety of bird life and come to know by sight some of the water and shore birds of eastern North America.

How to use this guide

Birds don't stay in one place for very long, so it is important to learn a few simple rules to help you quickly identify them. Most often what you see is a feeding or flying bird. If it is on the water one can watch to see if it dives, skims the surface or tips its head under water leaving its tail feathers pointing to the sky. If it is flying you can observe the beating pattern of its wings — are they quick wingbeats, is it soaring, does it flap its wings and then glide? The visual keys given in this guide focus on the principal features of each bird, namely, colour, outline, size, flying pattern and feeding style. The secondary features are found in the description. These include habitat, colour details and variations, shape of the head and the bill, and other identifying characteristics.

When you are looking at a bird, first estimate the size, then take note of the shape of the wings, tail, head, bill and feet. Note any particular marks — patches, streaks, stripes and speckles. Finally, observe its movements.

Legend for visual keys

1 **Size identification** — the rectangle represents the page of this book, and the silhouette of the bird represents its actual size against the page.

2 **Foot type** —

Tridactyl Anisodactyl

3 **Flight characteristics** —

Quick wingbeats

Slow steady wingbeats

Soaring

Wingbeats followed by gliding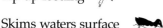

4 **Feeding technique** —

Stabs and prodding motion

Grazing and dabbling

Diving and clutching with feet

Diving head first

Dives from waters surface

Tip up feeding

Skims waters surface

5 **Egg** — Nova Scotia nesters only (actual size and shape unless other is indicated)

6 **Observation calendar** — the bar gives the initial for each month of the year. The colour indicates the best months for seeing the species, according to known migration patterns.

Observation Calendar
J F M A M J J A S O N D

Size Identification

Foot Type

Flying

Feeding

Egg: Actual Size

Nova Scotia Birding
HOT SPOTS

Lighthouse Route

1 **Little Port l'Hebert**

Salt marshes, sand flats, cobblestone beaches and uninhabited islands offer excellent nesting grounds for various gulls, Common Eider, guillemots and cormorants. Take exit 23 off Highway 103 and turn right at Sable River to Little Port l'Hebert. Parking available.

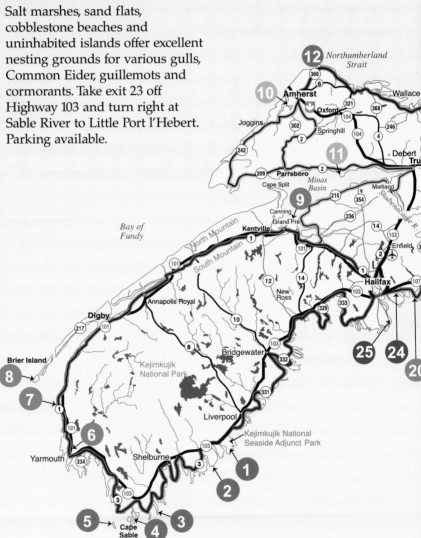

SCENIC TRAILS

- Cabot Trail
- Evangeline Trail
- Fleur-de-lys Trail
- Glooscap Trail
- Halifax and Dartmouth
- Lighthouse Route
- Marconi Trail
- Marine Drive
- Sunrise Trail

CAPE BRETON ISLAND

Pleasant Bay

Cape Breton Highlands National Park

Cheticamp

Ingonish

16

17

Margaree Harbour

162

Inverness

Glace Bay

223 · 125 · **Sydney**

Baddeck

327 · 255

Donkin

22

19

Bras d'Or Lake · 4

Big Pond

Louisbourg

105

13

15 · 245

337

St. Peters

4 · 104

247

Atlantic Ocean

Canso Causeway

104

Pictou

Antigonish

256

104

18

19

14 · 247

7 · 316

344

206

289

316

Canso

16

316

Sherbrooke · 211

23

224

7

Sheet Harbour

22

21

2 Black Point

This area has a variety of habitats — woodland, swamp, meadow, coastal and riverbank. Sea and shore birds are abundant, including eiders, terns and ducks. Take exit 23 off Highway 103, at Sable River, and follow the signs east toward the ocean. Park at Black Point Beach.

3 Blanche Cove

The salt marshes, beaches and woodlands on this peninsula offer a spectacular variety of birding opportunities. The area is a gathering ground for many migrating birds, such as sea ducks. Easy hiking trails will take you to the end of the peninsula in less than 30 minutes. Take exit 28 off Highway 103, at Clyde River, and follow signs to Blanche and Jenny's Point.

4 Cape Sable Island

Beautiful dunes and shoreline offer some very good birding, especially during migration seasons. There are opportunities here for spotting rare birds and transient visitors. Take exit 29 off Highway 103 at Barrington. Follow signs to Cape Sable Island, Clarks Harbour and The Hawk. The information centre in Clarks Harbour can direct you to specific locations and boat trips to Cape Sable.

5 Seal Island

This is considered one of the best locations on the Atlantic coast for sea birds. A two-hour boat trip from Clarks Harbour takes you to the island (see above for directions to Clarks Harbour). The Nova Scotia Bird Society organizes many such trips.

Evangeline Trail
6 Chebogue Meadows

These marsh and beach areas are perfect for spotting a variety of sea and shore birds including mergansers, ducks, Kingfishers, Osprey and many others. It is also especially good for observing migrating birds in spring and fall. Take Highway 101 north from Yarmouth.

7 Mavillette Beach

This provincial park includes salt marsh and beach areas where you may observe sandpipers, plovers, Willet, ducks, Blue Heron and many other sea and shore birds. Take Highway 101 north from Yarmouth to Mavillette.

3 Brier Island

This is one of the prime areas for birding in Nova Scotia. Shorebird activity throughout the spring, summer and fall includes sandpipers, Short-billed Dowitcher, yellowlegs, Sanderling and plovers. Also some interesting inland birds can be observed here. Take Highway 217 along Digby Neck. This trip includes two ferry rides.

9 Evangeline Beach/Minas Basin

The Bay of Fundy is one of the richest areas for bird watching both resident and transient species. Minas Basin, at the northeast end of the bay, is a provincial wildlife management area because of the spring and fall migrations. Thousands of birds gather on the beaches to feed. One of the most accessible places is Evangeline Beach near Wolfville. Take exit 10 off Highway 101 and follow signs.

Glooscap Trail

⑩ Amherst Point Migratory Sanctuary

From spring to fall this area has an abundance of sea and shore birds, including northern shovelers, black terns, rails, and bitterns. Marshes in the area offer excellent breeding grounds. Take exit 3 at Amherst off Highway 104 and follow the posted signs to the sanctuary.

⑪ Five Islands Provincial Park

This camping park has a spectacular range of habitats. Very high cliffs rise from the beach, giving a view of the islands and an estuary. When the tide is out the mudflats provide a large feeding ground for migrating birds. Inland trails also offer excellent hiking and interesting birdwatching. Take exit 11 off Highway 104 at Glenholme. Follow the signs for Parrsboro and Five Islands.

Sunrise Trail

⑫ Missaguash Marsh

The wetlands near the New Brunswick border are busy throughout the migration seasons. Thousands of birds move through the area including herons, bitterns, rails, sandpipers, grebes, and pintails with some rare spotting opportunities. The dykes allow for easy hiking. Take exit 1 off Highway 104 north of Amherst.

⑬ Caribou Provincial Park

This marsh and beach area is a favourite nesting and feeding ground for herons and ducks. There are opportunities for spotting rare and unusual species. Exit 22 (Highway 106) off Highway 104 to Pictou and follow signs to Route 6 and Caribou Island.

14 Melmerby Beach Provincial Park

This long sandbar has boardwalks for safe walking through the marshes and dunes. There are many species of shore birds here, including plovers, yellowlegs, sandpipers, sanderlings, and willet. Take exit 25 or 27A off Highway 104 to Shore Road.

15 Merigomish Island

This long spit of land has sheltered harbour on one side and the Northumberland Strait on the other. The feeding grounds at low tide are great places to see some rare birds, including the endangered Piping Plover. Take exit 27 off Highway 104 toward Merigomish. Best viewing is during spring and fall migration seasons.

Cape Breton
16 Bird Island

A boat is the only means of conveyance to reach this spectacular birdwatching location. This rocky island is a breeding ground for the Atlantic Puffin and many other sea birds. Boat tours leave from Big Bras d'Or. Take exit 15 off Highway 105.

17 Glace Bay Sanctuary

Ocean, salt marshes and

beaches offer excellent sightings of terns, Blue Heron, ducks, cormorants, gulls, Willet and many other species. Take exit 28 off Highway 4 near Glace Bay. No signs are posted so it is best to ask for directions on your arrival in the area.

18 Isle Madame

This island provides good birdwatching opportunities. The shoreline offers feeding grounds for shore birds while the lakes and woods are home to a variety of inland species. Take Route 320 to the island which can be reached by causeway from Highway 104 at Louisdale.

19 Point Michaud Provincial Park

Situated on the Atlantic Ocean, this park has a beautiful beach with sand dunes. A system of ponds nearby offers additional birdwatching opportunities. Take Route 247 east from St. Peters.

Marine Drive
20 Fox Point

A wonderful area within easy reach of the city for an opportunity to see Common Eider, Piping Plover, Blue Heron, ducks, scoters and many other shore birds. Walk the beach or hike the trails through meadows and sea grass along marshes. Take Route 207 out of Dartmouth towards Lawrencetown area. Turn right on Conrad Road and proceed to the beach parking lot.

21 Martinique Beach Provincial Park

This is a very long beach with dunes and saltmarsh and is adjacent to a bird sanctuary. It is an excellent location for a variety of species, all year round. Canada Geese are in abundance during the migration periods. Take Route 7 (Highway 107) out of Dartmouth to Musquodoboit Harbour. Turn right on Petpeswick Road which ends at the beach.

22 Taylor Head Provincial Park

This hiking area and beach offer birdwatching of many different kinds. The woods and fields are home to many inland species. Along the rocky shore, the beach and the sheltered parts of the shoreline one can see a variety of shore and sea birds. Take Route 7 from Dartmouth. At Spry Bay follow signs to the park.

23 Tor Bay Provincial Park

At one of the most easterly points of mainland Nova Scotia is Tor Bay with its white sand beaches and rocky headlands. Many species of sea birds can be seen here, including some rare and transient birds. Take Route 16 to Guysborough and follow signs to Larrys River.

Halifax Regional Municipality

24 Cole Harbour Preservation Area

A beautiful walk takes you along the old railroad, now part of the Trans-Canada Trail. You can see gulls, terns, cormorants, Osprey and many other species in this sheltered saltwater area. Take Route 207 to Cole Harbour and turn down Bissett Road. There are two parking lots.

25 Duncans Cove

There are popular hiking trails here along a rocky shore. The many species of shore birds in this area make for great birdwatching. Take Route 349 out of Halifax and turn left on Duncans Cove Road. Parking is available on the side of the road.

American Bittern

Botaurus lentiginosus

Size Identification

Foot: Anisodactyl

Flying

Feeding

Observation Calendar

J F M A M J J A S O N D

Male/Female: Overall reddish brown with white stripes on underside; yellow bill long and sharp; short brown tail lightly banded; smudgy brown back. In flight: Tips of wings dark brown.

Did you know? The American Bittern is extremely difficult to spot in the field because, if approached, it will freeze and blend into the reeds.

Voice: In flight, a loud *squark*. Song is a loud *kong-chu-chunk*, on breeding grounds.
Food: Small fish, reptiles, amphibians, insects, small mammals.
Nest/Eggs: Concealed platform built from aquatic plants just above water. 2-6 eggs.

Egg: Actual Size

Double-crested Cormorant

Phalacrocorax auritus

Foot: Tridactyl

Observation Calendar

J F M A M J J A S O N D

Male/Female: Overall black with long tail feathers; bright orange chin and throat patch, feet and legs black. Crest is visible only during courtship. In flight: Neck is kinked.

Did you know? Cormorants are often seen perched on a rock or pier with wings fully extended to dry their feathers.

Often seen flying extremely high.

Voice: Call is a variety of grunts and croaks, only at its nest. Elsewhere silent.
Food: Small fish.
Nest/Eggs: Colonies. Platform built of sticks and twigs lined with leaves, grass and placed on ground or small tree. 3-5 eggs.

Flying

Feeding

Egg: Actual Size

17

Cormorants

Size Identification

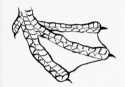

Foot: Tridactyl

Flying

Feeding

Great Cormorant

Phalacrocorax carbo

Observation Calendar

J F M A M J J A S O N D

Male/Female: Overall black with large grey bill hooked at end; yellow where bill meets the throat, white cheeks and throat; black feet and legs. Larger than Double-crested Cormorant.

Did you know? Cormorants will fly in V-formations in small flocks and are silent in flight.

Voice: Variety of grunt-like calls and a croak only at its nest. Elsewhere silent.
Food: Many different types of fish.
Nest/Eggs: Colonies. Platform of sticks lined with seaweed on rocky ledge near water or isolated on an island. 3-4 eggs.

Egg: Actual Size

Dovekie

Alle alle

Observation Calendar

J F M A M J J A S O N D

Male/Female: Small black head and back, short stout black bill, small white line above eye; white belly; feet and legs black; short black tail. *Winter:* Chin and throat turn white. In flight: Very quick wing beats that are often blurred.

Spends most of its time on the open ocean.

Voice: Variety of chattering and squeaking notes.
Food: Crustaceans, plankton.

Short-billed Dowitcher

Limnodromus griseus

Observation Calendar

J F M A M J J A S O N D

Male/Female: *Summer*: Rust neck and chest speckled black; back and wings dark brown speckled with buff; dark brown cap on head. *Winter*: Grey speckled overall with dark, barred flanks; black bill fading to yellow near base, white eyebrows; black and brown tail feathers; feet and legs yellow.

Voice: Call is *tu*, repeated several times in soft high-pitch.
Food: Marine worms, molluscs, insects.

American Black Duck

Anas rubripes

Foot: Tridactyl

Flying

Feeding

Observation Calendar
J F M A M J J A S O N D

Male: Dark black with hint of brown overall and blue speculum; bill is olive; feet and legs orange. In flight: White patches under wings.
Female: Overall lighter brown than male with orange and black bill.

Voice: Both female and male *quack*. Male also whistles.
Food: Vegetation, insects, amphibians, snails, seed, grain, berries.
Nest/Eggs: Depression on ground lined with grass, leaves and down, close to water's edge. 8-12 eggs.

Egg: Actual Size

21

Blue-winged Teal
Anas discors

Observation Calendar

J F M A M J J A S O N D

Male: Grey head with crescent shaped white patch running up face, bill black; chest and belly brown; back and wings dark brown with buff highlights; blue and green speculum; feet and legs yellow.
Female: Overall brown speckled with pale blue speculum.

Voice: Male has high pitched *peeeep*. Female — *quack* is soft high-pitch.
Food: Aquatic plants, seeds.
Nest/Eggs: Pile of grasses lined with down, close to waters edge, concealed. 9-12 eggs.

Bufflehead
Bucephala albeola

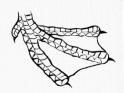
Foot: Tridactyl

Flying

Feeding

Observation Calendar
J F M A M J J A S O N D

Male: Small compact duck; black head with large white patch behind the eye, grey bill; black back with white underparts.
Female: Grey-brown overall with smaller white patch behind the eye.

Voice: Mostly quiet. Male whistles. Female quacks.
Food: Small fish, crustaceans, molluscs and snails.

Common Goldeneye
Bucephala clangula

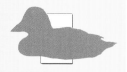

Observation Calendar

J F M A M J J A S O N D

Male: Black/green head with round white patch on cheek, close to black bill; back black with white bars; underside white; orange feet and legs. In flight: Large white speculum. **Female:** Brown head and light charcoal overall; bill black with yellow patch; white patches on back. Both male and female are stocky with large head.

Voice: Call during courtship *jeeeeent*. Wings whistle when in flight. Female — low grating sound in flight.
Food: Molluscs, crustaceans, aquatic insects.
Nest/Eggs: In tree cavity or built structure lined with down. 8-12 eggs.

Green-winged Teal

Anas crecca

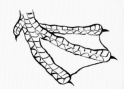

Foot: Tridactyl

Flying

Observation Calendar
J F M A M J J A S O N D

Feeding

Male: Head is rust with green patch running around eye to back of head, bill black, black at back of base of neck; warm grey body with thin black banding; distinctive white bar running down side just in front of wing; white rump; short square tail.

Female: Overall dull brown with green speculum; dark band running through eye.

Voice: Male — high pitched whistle. Female — weak shrill voice.

Food: Seeds, aquatic plants, corn, wheat, oats.

Nest/Eggs: On ground, cup shaped, filled with grasses and weeds, sometimes a distance from water. 10-12 eggs.

Egg: Actual Size

25

Harlequin Duck

Hiostrionicus histrionicus

Size Identification

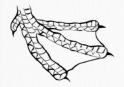

Foot: Tridactyl

Flying

Feeding

Observation Calendar

J F M A M J J A S O N D

Male: Blue-grey head with white patch behind bill running up forehead; black bill; white ear patch. Black stripe on crown with chestnut brown on either side; white collar band and white patch on side of breast; chestnut brown sides; blue-grey back; black tail; feet and legs grey; small tail feathers. In flight: Long tail revealed; dark belly.

Female: Overall dark brown; white patches on face and behind eye; grey bill. In flight: White belly.

Voice: Male — high-pitched whistles. Female — agitated *ekekekek* and also *quacks*.
Food: Insects, molluscs.

Mallard

Anas platyrhynchos

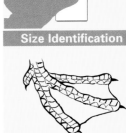

Foot: Tridactyl

Flying

Feeding

Observation Calendar

J F M A M J J A S O N D

Male: Bright green iridescent head, yellow bill; thin white collar; chestnut brown chest; grey sides; black and grey back; white tail; black curled feathers over rump; feet and legs orange. In flight: blue speculum with white border, underparts of wings grey and brown.
Female: Overall brown streaked with orange bill, black patches on bill; white tail feathers.

Voice: Male — call soft *raeb* repeated. Female — loud *quacks* repeated.
Food: Aquatic plants, grain, insects.
Nest/Eggs: Shallow cup built of grasses and aquatic plants lined with feathers on ground concealed near water. 8-10 eggs.

Egg: Actual Size

27

Northern Shoveler

Anas clypeata

Observation Calendar

J F M A M J J A S O N D

Male: Grey speckled head and neck; yellow eye; wide black bill; sides rust; mottled brown back. In flight: Green speculum; light blue wing patch.
Female: Overall brown with orange bill.

Voice: Low *quack* or *cluck*.
Food: Aquatic plants, duckweed, insects.
Nest/Eggs: Made from grasses in hollow on ground lined with down feathers at a distance from water. 8-12 eggs.

Oldsquaw
Clangula hyemalis

Foot: Tridactyl

Flying

Feeding

Observation Calendar
J F M A M J J A S O N D

Male: *Winter*: White head with grey cheek and black patch; bill black with tan band; white back with black and tan markings; black chest and white belly; very long tail feathers.
Female: *Winter*: White face, black crown; back brown with black wings; chest brown and white belly.

Did you know? This duck is also named Long-tailed Duck.

Voice: Male — call during courtship sounds similar to yodelling. Female — soft grunting and quacking.
Food: Insect larvae, molluscs, crustaceans.

29

Ring-necked Duck
Aythya collaris

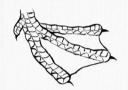

Observation Calendar

J F M A M J J A S O N D

Male: Back, head and breast black, high forehead; black bill with white outlines; yellow eyes; white spur on breast leading to grey underside and belly. In flight: Grey speculum; white belly.
Female: Grey cheeks and bill; one white band at tip of bill; white eye ring; dark charcoal back; brown chest, belly and sides.

Voice: Male has low, loud whistle. Female call is soft *prrrrrrrrr* notes. Mostly quiet.
Food: Aquatic plants, molluscs, insects.
Nest/Eggs: Cup-shaped, built of grasses and moss and lined with down feathers, concealed near pond. 8-12 eggs.

Wood Duck

Aix sponsa

Foot: Tridactyl

Flying

Feeding

Observation Calendar

J F M A M J J A S O N D

Male: Green head and drooping crest; black cheeks; red eye and white throat with two spurs; bill orange with black markings; chest brown with white spots leading to white belly; black and green back; sides tan with white and black band. In flight: Long squared tail.

Female: Back and crown brown; white eye ring; speckled breast and lighter coloured belly.

Voice: Male — high-pitch whistle. Female — loud *oooooeeek* in flight.

Food: Aquatic plants, insects, minnows, amphibians.

Nest/Eggs: In cavity of tree, as high as 20 metres, or in a log or built structure lined with wood chips and feathers. 9-12 eggs.

Egg: Actual Size

Dunlin
Calidris alpina

Size Identification

Foot: Anisodactyl

Flying

Feeding

Observation Calendar

J F M A M J J A S O N D

Male/Female: Long black bill; grey face with rust and black speckled crown; breast white speckled brown; dull brown wings and back; short black tail; feet and legs black. In flight: White underparts and wing feathers.

Did you know? Dunlins usually flock together performing wonderful aerial shows when flushed.

Voice: In flight call: soft *creeeep* or *chit-lit*.
Food: Crustaceans, molluscs, marine worms, insects.

Common Eider

Somateria mollissima

Foot: Tridactyl

Flying

Feeding

J F M A M J J A S O N D

Male: Large black patch on crown; white face; pale grey-green on back of head and from crown to beak. Overall white with black tail, belly and sides. In flight: Wing feathers black.
Female: Overall speckled brown with dark brown on head; bill grey; tail feathers often cocked.

Voice: Male *coooos* during courtship. Female — deep hoarse-sounding *quack*.
Food: Sea urchins, molluscs, crustaceans.
Nest/Eggs: Built of aquatic plants, moss and grasses lined with down feathers placed on ground, preferably rocky terrain. 3-5 eggs.

Egg: 90%

Northern Fulmar
Fulmarus glacialis

Flying

Feeding

Observation Calendar

J F M A M J J A S O N D

Male/Female: Plumage varies from light grey with white head, breast and underparts to overall grey with darker back; large thick neck with white rounded forehead; bill is yellow with banding; dark wing tips.

Voice: Occasional loud *quack* similar to a duck when aggressive. Quiet.
Food: Small fish, jellyfish, squid and shrimp from water's surface.

Northern Gannet

Morus bassanus

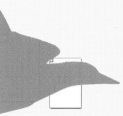

Size Identification

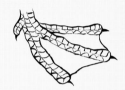

Foot: Tridactyl

Flying

Feeding

Observation Calendar

J F M A M J J A S O N D

Male/Female: Overall white with black wing tips; pale yellow on side of head; broad grey bill; yellow eye surrounded by black eye ring.

Did you know? When Northern Gannets dive, they fold their wings, becoming like arrowheads. When you see Northern Gannets feeding it is a clue that whales may also be in the area chasing schools of fish.

Voice: Low croaks and grunts, during courtship.
Food: Schooling fish including mackerel and herring.

Egg: 80%

Canada Goose
Branta canadensis

Size Identification

Foot: Tridactyl

Flying

Feeding

Observation Calendar

J F M A M J J A S O N D

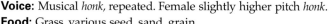

Male/Female: Black head, neck and bill; white cheek patch; breast and belly pale brown with white flecks; feet and legs black; back and wings brown with white edging; short black tail; white rump, seen in flight. In flight: Flies in "V" formations.

Voice: Musical *honk*, repeated. Female slightly higher pitch *honk*.
Food: Grass, various seed, sand, grain.
Nest/Eggs: Large nest of twigs, moss and grass lined with down feathers placed near water's edge. 4-8 eggs.

Egg: 75%

36

Pied-billed Grebe

Podilymbus podiceps

Size Identification

Foot: Tridactyl

Flying

Feeding

Observation Calendar

J F M A M J J A S O N D

Male/Female: *Summer*: Overall brown with grey-brown back; yellow eye ring; stout bill, white with distinct black band; black chin; short tail. *Winter*: White ring on bill softens; lighter chin. White tail feathers occasionally revealed when threatened by another bird. In flight: white patch on belly and white trail edge on wings.

Voice: Call is *cow* repeated with *keeech* at end, also various cluckings.
Food: Small fish, amphibians, crayfish, aquatic insects.
Nest/Eggs: Platform built with aquatic plants in shallow water attached to reeds and other aquatic plants. 5-7 eggs.

Egg: Actual Size

Red-necked Grebe
Podiceps grisegena

Observation Calendar

J F M A M J J A S O N D

Male/Female: *Summer*: Black crown with white cheeks and chin; long thick neck is rust blending to black back and wings; bill is broad yellow and black. *Winter*: Loses all colour except black and grey; bill remains yellow. In flight: white underwings and belly, and white edges on wings.

Voice: Chattering, squeaks and long notes on breeding grounds. Quiet in winter.
Food: Small fish, aquatic insects, marine worms, molluscs, crustaceans.

Black Guillemot
Cepphus grylle

Observation Calendar

J F M A M J J A S O N D

Male/Female: Black overall with white oval patch on wing; feet and legs orange; bill is black with bright red inside mouth. *Winter*: White head, chest and belly. In flight: White under wings.

Voice: High pitched *squeaks*.
Food: Fish and crustaceans.
Nest/Eggs: On ground and in cracks on cliffs, concealed by driftwood, sticks and boulders. 1-2 eggs.

Common Black-headed Gull

Larus ridibundus

Size Identification

Foot: Tridactyl

Flying

Feeding

Observation Calendar

J F M A M J J A S O N D

Male/Female: *Summer*: Brown head that may appear black in early spring; white eye ring; thin red bill; neck chest and belly white; back and wings soft grey with black wing tips; white rump; black tail; feet and legs red. In flight: Tips of white wings blend to charcoal outlined in white.

Voice: Call is high-pitched harsh *uuup* and various squeals.
Food: Insects, earthworms and small fish.

Glaucous Gull
Larus hyperboreus

Foot: Tridactyl

Flying

Observation Calendar

J F M A M J J A S O N D

Feeding

Male/Female: Overall white with light grey back and wings; bill is yellow with red patch on lower portion at tip; yellow eye; pink legs and feet; short square white tail. In flight: White wing tips on grey wings.

Voice: Variety of squawks and other calls that are deep and hoarse sounding.

Food: Small mammals, birds, eggs, insects, garbage, small fish, crustaceans, carrion, molluscs.

Great Black-backed Gull

Larus marinus

Foot: Tridactyl

Flying

Observation Calendar

J F M A M J J A S O N D

Feeding

Male/Female: White head, chin, chest and belly, red patch on lower portion of bill; feet and legs pink / grey; black wings with thin white band on trailing edge; tail and back black.
In flight: Pale grey undersides with black wing tip; tail white.

Voice: Loud squawks and deep guttural notes.
Food: Scavenger. Small fish, mammals, young birds and garbage. Major predator of other birds including puffin and tern chicks.
Nest/Eggs: Colonies. Mound of seaweed and other coastal plants lined with grasses on ground or rocky ledge. 3 eggs.

Egg: 80%

Herring Gull

Larus argentatus

Observation Calendar

J F M A M J J A S O N D

Male/Female: White head that in winter is streaked light brown; yellow eye and bill; small red patch on lower bill; tail black; feet and legs red. In flight: Grey wing with white on trailing edge and black tips; pale brown rump; wide charcoal tail feathers.

Voice: Variety of squawks and squeals. Aggressive alarm call is *kak kak kak kak* ending in *yucca*.
Food: Insects, small mammals, clams, fish, small birds, crustaceans, mussels, rodents, garbage.
Nest/Eggs: Colonies. Mound lined with grass and seaweed on ground or cliff. Usually on islands. 2-4 eggs.

Iceland Gull

Larus glaucoides kumlieni

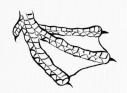

Observation Calendar

J F M A M J J A S O N D

Male/Female: Overall white with light grey back and wings; white wings underside; yellow bill with red tip on lower part; yellow eye; dark pink feet and legs. In flight: Overall white and grey underparts; white patches on wing tips.

Voice: Mostly quiet. Variety of squeaks.
Food: Fish, carrion, bird eggs.

Lesser Black-backed Gull

Larus fuscus

Observation Calendar

J F M A M J J A S O N D

Male/Female: Mostly white head with light brown streaking, yellow eye; yellow bill with small red patch; dark grey back and wings; black wing tips; feet and legs yellow. In flight: pale grey underparts; white on trailing edge of wing; black wing tip with small white spot.

Voice: Low pitched squawks and squeals.
Food: Insects, small birds, small mammals. Notable for stealing food from other gulls.

Ring-billed Gull
Larus delawarensis

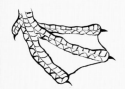

Observation Calendar

J F M A M J J A S O N D

Male/Female: *Summer*: White overall; yellow bill with black band at end; yellow eye; pale grey wings and black tips and white patches within black tips; black feet and legs. *Winter*: Feet and legs turn yellow; light brown spots on top of head and back of neck. In flight: grey underparts; black wing tips.

Voice: Loud *kaawk* and other calls.
Food: Insects, bird eggs, worms, garbage.
Nest/Eggs: Colonies. Grasses, sticks, twigs and pebbles built on ground. 3 eggs.

Great Blue Heron

Ardea herodias

Foot: Anisodactyl

Flying

Feeding

Observation Calendar
J F M A M J J A S O N D

Male/Female: Overall grey-blue with black crest on top of head; long neck and bill; black patch connecting eye and long yellow bill; white head; long grey legs and feet; long feathers extend over wings and base of neck. In flight: Neck is kinked; legs extend past tail; constant wing flapping with occasional glide.

Voice: Bill makes clacking sound. Call is harsh *squawk*.
Food: Small fish, reptiles, amphibians, crustaceans, birds, aquatic insects.
Nest/Eggs: Colonies. Platform of aquatic plants and twigs lined with softer materials such as down and soft grass, placed in tree or shrub. 3-7 eggs.

Egg: Actual Size

Parasitic Jaeger

Stercorarius parasiticus

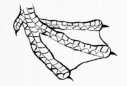

Observation Calendar

J F M A M J J A S O N D

Male/Female: Dark brown cap and mask; pale to white neck and breast. Some birds are brown all over. In flight: very long dark tail feathers; wings are "V" shaped; white patches on black underside of wing; pale belly with grey banding on breast.

Voice: Mostly quiet.
Food: Usually steals from gulls and terns.

Killdeer

Charadrius vociferus

Foot: Anisodactyl

Flying

Feeding

Observation Calendar
J F M A M J J A S O N D

Male/Female: Bright red eye with black band running across forehead; white chin, collar and eyebrow; black collar ring under white; black chest band set against white chest and belly; back and wing rust and grey; wing tipped in black; legs and feet pink/grey. In flight: Orange rump; black wing tips and white band on trailing edge.

Did you know? A killdeer will exhibit a "broken-wing" display when a predator comes close to the nest sight. The bird will appear hurt and run around distracting the predator from the nest.

Voice: Variety of calls with most common being *kill deeee* which is repeated.
Food: Insects.
Nest/Eggs: Hollow on ground with some pebbles. Most popular sightings in gravel parking lots. 3-4 eggs.

Egg: Actual Size

Belted Kingfisher
Ceryle alcyon

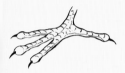

Observation Calendar
J F M A M J J A S O N D

Male: A large crested blue/black head and long black bill; wings black with white bands; chest white; white collar wraps around neck with blue band that wraps around chest; very short blue tail; feet and legs charcoal.
Female: Rust-coloured breast band.

Did you know? Belted Kingfishers teach their young to dive for food by catching a fish, stunning it, then placing it on the surface of the water. The young birds then practice diving for it.

Voice: A continuous deep rattle during flight.
Food: Small fish, amphibians, reptiles, insects and crayfish.
Nest/Eggs: A cavity or tunnel excavated in a bank near a river or lake. 5-8 eggs.

Black-legged Kittiwake

Rissa tricactyla

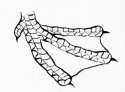

Observation Calendar

J F M A M J J A S O N D

Male/Female: White head, chest, belly and tail; bill yellow; wings grey with black triangular tips; feet and legs black. *Winter:* Dark grey patch behind eye. In flight: All grey upperparts of wings with black tips. Immature birds have large black patch on upper wings forming an "M" shape in flight.

Voice: Repetitive *kee* and *ketiwake*. Variety of notes.
Food: Small fish off surface of water.
Nest/Eggs: Colonies. Cup-shaped mud, seaweed and grass on rocky ledge or building. 2 eggs.

Red Knot

Calidris canutus

Observation Calendar

J F M A M J J A S O N D

Male/Female: *Winter:* Face, neck and chest turn from brick red in summer to light grey; wings and tail turn dark; black bill; legs and feet charcoal.

Did you know? Red Knots are mostly seen flying in flocks of hundreds of birds with Dunlins, plovers, Godwits, sandpipers and many other shorebirds in their migration south or north.

Voice: Call is low *nuuuut*. Soft *currret* in flight.
Food: Molluscs, worms, insects, crabs, seeds.

Common Loon
Gavia immer

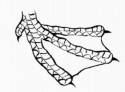

Size Identification

Foot: Tridactyl

Flying

Observation Calendar

J F M A M J J A S O N D

Feeding

Male/Female: *Summer*: Black head and neck with white banded neck ring; thick grey sharp bill; red eye; white chest and belly; black back and wings spotted white; feet and legs black. *Winter*: Contrasting blacks and whites muted to dark dull brown. In flight: Large feet trail behind tail feathers; quick wing beats close to water's surface; takes off from water by running across surface.

Did you know? Loons can remain underwater for more than 5 minutes. They dive to feed and to avoid danger.

Voice: Drawn out *lou-lou-lou-lou* like yodelling, often at dusk or dawn.
Food: Small fish.
Nest/Eggs: Mound built with aquatic plants, mostly on islands. 2 eggs.

Egg: 75%

Red-throated Loon

Gavia stellata

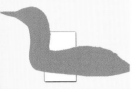

Observation Calendar

J F M A M J J A S O N D

Male/Female: *Winter*: Face changes from grey to white; red throat becomes white; grey speckled head; bill grey; white speckles on black back, white belly. In flight: Only loon capable of take off from land; quick wing beats over surface of water.

Voice: When breeding, a variety of high-pitched calls, but quieter than common loon.
Food: Small fish.

Common Merganser
Mergus merganser

Observation Calendar

J F M A M J J A S O N D

Male: Dark green head crested with red toothed bill slightly hooked at end; white ring around neck connects to white chest and belly; black back and white sides; feet and legs orange.
Female: Brown head and grey-brown back; white chin.

Voice: Male call is *twaang*. Female call is series of hard notes.
Food: Small fish, crustaceans and molluscs.
Nest/Eggs: Built of reeds and grass and lined with down feathers in tree cavity, rock crevice, on ground or in built structure. 8-11 eggs.

Hooded Merganser
Lophodytes cucullatus

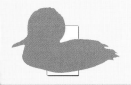

Foot: Tridactyl

Flying

Feeding

Observation Calendar

J F M A M J J A S O N D

Male: Black crested head with large white patch on back of head behind eye; black bill is long and thin; rust eye; black back with rust sides and white underparts; black band runs down side into chest; white bands on black wings; tail is often cocked. In flight: Rapid energetic wing beats.
Female: Grey breast and belly; faint rust on back of crest; wings dark brown.

Voice: Call is low croaking or *gack*.
Food: Small fish, reptiles, crustaceans, molluscs, and aquatic insects.
Nest/Eggs: In tree cavity or built structure lined with grasses and down feathers, occasionally on ground. 9-12 eggs.

Egg: Actual Size

Red-breasted Merganser

Mergus serrator

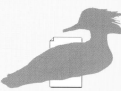

Size Identification

Foot: Tridactyl

Flying

Feeding

Observation Calendar
J F M A M J J A S O N D

Male: *Winter:* Dark green and black head with crest, red eye, white neck ring, long orange toothed bill with slight hook at end; chest white, spotted black; back black with white patching. *Summer:* Head chestnut brown; overall body grey. In flight: Rapid wing beats; straight flying pattern. Dark breast on male.
Female: Brown head with grey upper parts and white belly.

Voice: Call for male is *eoooow* usually during courtship. Female — series of hard notes. Mostly quiet.
Food: Small fish, molluscs, crustaceans.
Nest/Eggs: Built of grass and down in sheltered area under bush. 8-10 eggs.

Egg: Actual Size

57

Common Murre
Uria aalge

Observation Calendar

J F M A M J J A S O N D

Male/Female: *Summer*: Black overall with white chest and belly; long black bill; feet and legs black. *Winter*: White throat and cheeks; dark line through cheek. In flight: White underparts.

Did you know? The Murre is capable of diving down to depths of 100 metres or more.

Voice: Purr-like low *muurrrr* sounds similar to its name, also growls.
Food: Small fish.
Nest/Eggs: Colonies. No nest material except a few pebbles on a rocky ledge. Egg colours and patterns will vary. 1 egg.

Thick-billed Murre

Uria lomvia

Foot: Tridactyl

Flying

Feeding

Observation Calendar
J F M A M J J A S O N D

Male/Female: *Summer*: Black overall with white chest and belly; distinctive white line runs along edge of sharp bill; thin white bands on wings; feet and legs black. *Winter*: Dark greyish overall with white chin, cheeks, chest and belly. In flight: White belly.

Voice: Purr-like low *muurrrr* sounds similar to its name, also growls.
Food: Small fish.

Foot: Anisodactyl

Flying

Feeding

Egg: 70%

Osprey
Pandion haliaetus

Observation Calendar
J F M A M J J A S O N D

Male/Female: In flight: White belly and chest; wings grey with black banding; white wing underparts connect to chest; black band running through eye; large black bill; tail grey with black banding. Perched: Black back with wings with thin white line running above wing; eye yellow with black band running through and down to cheek; chin white; top of head white with black patches. Seen along Atlantic coastline, including Halifax Harbour.

Voice: A loud chirp which trails off or ascending *squeeee* during courtship displays.
Food: Various small fish.
Nest/Eggs: Constructed of twigs and sticks, lined with sod, grass and vines in upper parts of trees and on top of poles. 2-3 eggs.

Leach's Storm-Petrel

Oceanodroma leucorhoa

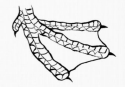

Observation Calendar

J F M A M J J A S O N D

Male/Female: Overall brown with black wing tips and tail; bill black; feet and legs black. In flight: Indirect flying pattern, cutting back and forth quickly; wings narrow and bent. White band on rump.

Voice: Call is high-pitched screams and trills during breeding. Quiet at sea.
Food: Small fish, squid, plankton.
Nest/Eggs: Hole in ground on islands along Atlantic coast.

Wilson's Storm-Petrel
Oceanites oceanicus

Observation Calendar

J F M A M J J A S O N D

Male/Female: Overall black and charcoal with "U" shaped white rump; black bill is hooked downward at end; black feet and legs. In flight: Flies straight with continuous wingbeats and occasional short glides.

Voice: Soft *peeep* when feeding.
Food: Small fish, plankton and squid at water's surface.

Red Phalarope

Phalaropus fulicaria

Size Identification

Foot: Anisodactyl

Flying

Feeding

Observation Calendar
J F M A M J J A S O N D

Male: *Summer*: Black cap and white mask over eye to back of head; yellow bill with black tip; body rust red with grey belly; wings brown with tan highlights.

Female: *Summer*: Bright yellow bill with black tip; black head with large white patch around eye to back of neck; long rufous neck, rufous chest, belly and sides; black back with white and rust highlights; rufous rump. In flight: White wing band on underside.

Male/Female: *Winter*: White and pale grey head, neck, breast and belly; back and wings grey; black mark over eye.

Voice: Call is high-pitched *wiiit* or *kreep*.
Food: Aquatic insects, small fish, crustaceans.

Red-necked Phalarope

Phalaropus lobatus

Observation Calendar
J F M A M J J A S O N D

Male/Female: *Winter:* White and grey chest and belly. Face white with black mark behind eye; dark grey wings and back.
Male: *Summer:* Top of head black; long black bill; white chin; black band running under eye against white and rust; rust neck; grey chest changing to white belly; dark brown and rust wings and back; tail black; white rump.
Female: Overall similar markings except bolder colour; and rufous neck with more contrast overall.

Voice: Call is sharp *twic*.
Food: Aquatic insects, molluscs, crustaceans.

Wilson's Phalarope

Phalaropus tricolor

Observation Calendar

J F M A M J J A S O N D

Male: *Summer*: White throat; light rust on back of head changing to pale grey on breast; pale grey underparts; grey back and wings.

Female: *Summer*: Long thin black bill, white chin and cheeks turning rust running down white neck; black band runs from beak through eye down side of neck to back; grey cap; white sides and belly; grey feet and legs. In flight: White rump; no wing bands; long legs.

Male/Female: *Winter*: Similar to summer male with pale grey, not rust, on head and neck.

Did you know? This is one species where the male does all the nest tending. He builds the nest, incubates eggs and raises young.

Voice: Soft call is *aangh*.
Food: Insects, crustaceans.
Nest/Eggs: Colonies. Hollow scrap on ground lined with grasses and concealed in grass. 4 eggs.

Northern Pintail

Anas acuta

Size Identification

Foot:

Flying

Feeding

Observation Calendar
J F M A M J J A S O N D

Male: Brown head with white line circling around cheeks to chest; white chest and belly; back and wings are black and grey; long tail is black and brown; rump black; sides grey with thin black banding; bill grey with white line. In flight: Long tail; white neck and line running up neck.
Female: Overall brown with black bill; no pintail feature.

Voice: Male has 2 high-pitched whistles. Female quacks.
Food: Aquatic plants, seeds, crustaceans, corn, grains.
Nest/Eggs: Bowl of sticks, twigs, grasses and lined with down at a distance from water's edge. 6-9 eggs.

Egg: 90%

American Golden-Plover

Pluvialis dominica

Foot: Anisodactyl

Flying

Feeding

Observation Calendar
J F M A M J J A S O N D

Male/Female: *Summer*: Crown, back of neck, back and wings black or dark grey strongly speckled with yellow; black face mask running into breast and black belly and rump; white runs from forehead down side of neck to chest; grey legs.
Winter: Strong contrasting colours change to soft grey on face, head, chest and belly. Yellow speckles are muted.
In flight: Dark underwings; grey patch on inner wing near body.

Voice: Call is soft *kuee-leee*.
Food: Molluscs, aquatic insects, marine worms.

Black-bellied Plover
Pluvialis squatarola

Observation Calendar
J F M A M J J A S O N D

Male/Female: *Summer*: Black mask set against pale grey speckled head, crown and neck; bill black; breast and belly black; wings and tail black with white speckles; white rump; feet and legs black. *Winter*: Black face patch; dull grey-brown chest and belly. In flight: Black on inner wings underparts; white wing band; white rump.

Voice: Call is whistled 3-note *pee oo ee*.
Food: Marine worms, insects, crustaceans, molluscs, seeds.

Piping Plover

Charadrius melodus

Observation Calendar

J F M A M J J A S O N D

Male/Female: *Spring and Summer*: Light greyish upperparts with distinctive black band across forehead; bill yellow with black tip; black collar; white chin, cheeks, chest and belly; black wing feathers; feet and legs yellow.
Winter: Black collar band becomes grey; bill black.
In flight: Quick wingbeats with slight glide just before landing; white at base of tail and black tail feathers.

Did you know? The Piping Plover is an endangered species and its nesting grounds are under special protection.

Voice: Call is soft whistled *peeeep*.
Food: Insect larvae, molluscs, crustaceans, fly larvae and marine worms.
Nest/Eggs: Scraped out hollow on sand with a few pebbles or shells. 3-4 eggs.

Semipalmated Plover
Charadrius semipalmatus

Observation Calendar
J F M A M J J A S O N D

Male/Female: *Summer*: Dark brown head, back and wings; small white patch on forehead with black band above; faint white eyebrow; white chin extending into white collar with black collar band below; chest and belly white; wing feathers black; feet and legs orange; bill is orange tipped in black.
In flight: Quick wingbeats with slight glide just before landing.

Voice: Whistle *chee-weee* with a defensive call in quick short notes. Also soft rattling.
Food: Marine worms.
Nest/Eggs: Hollow on ground with shell bits and grass on sand or gravel. 4 eggs.

Atlantic Puffin

Fratercula artica

Foot: Tridactyl

Flying

Feeding

Observation Calendar

J F M A M J J A S O N D

Male/Female: *Summer*: Only puffin in eastern regions. Large colourful bill with white mask; black collar, head and back; white chest and belly; orange eye ring; wings and tail black; orange feet and legs. *Winter*: Markings slightly duller.

Voice: Hard sounding *urrrr* and croaks.
Food: Small fish, crustaceans and squid.
Nest/Eggs: Colonies. A rock crevice under boulder lined with grasses or a burrow dug in soft sand. 1 egg.

Egg: Actual Size

71

Virginia Rail
Rallus limicola

Foot: Anisodactyl

Flying

Feeding

Observation Calendar

J F M A M J J A S O N D

Male/Female: Chicken-like; grey head banded dark charcoal on top; eye red; neck and sides rich rust; long curved red and black bill; back dark brown with rust edging; wings rust with black; short black and brown tail; legs and feet red; belly black and white banding.

Voice: Call is descending *kicket* repeated with grunting notes.
Food: Marine worms, snails, aquatic insects.
Nest/Eggs: Cup built of grass and reeds built slightly above water's surface attached to reeds and other aquatic plant life. 5-12 eggs.

Egg: Actual Size

Yellow Rail

Coturnicops noveboracensis

J F M A M J J A S O N D

Male/Female: Chicken-like; dark band running across top of head to back; thick yellow bill; dark brown running through eye; buff face, breast and belly; dark brown and buff on back and wings with white bars. In flight: White patch on edge of wings.

Voice: Call a progressive *click click click* similar to tapping two stones together.
Food: Snails, insects, seeds.
Nest/Eggs: Well concealed cup built into grass or attached to stems slightly above water level. 7-10 eggs.

Size Identification

Foot: Anisodactyl

Flying

Feeding

Egg: Actual Size

Razorbill
Alca torda

Size Identification

Foot: Tridactyl

Flying

Feeding

Egg: 90%

Observation Calendar
J F M A M J J A S O N D

Male/Female: Black head, neck and back with white line running under eye to top of bill; bill black with white and grey lines running down to tip; chest and belly white; feet and legs black; black wings and pointed tail feathers are often cocked; thick neck.

Did you know? The Razorbill can dive down 100 metres and stay under water for almost a minute.

Voice: Various croak-like sounds and growls.
Food: Small fish.
Nest/Eggs: Colonies. Twigs placed on rocky ledge or in burrow between boulders, but sometimes no nest built. 1 egg.

Sanderling

Calidris alba

Size Identification

Foot: Anisodactyl

Flying

Feeding

Observation Calendar

J F M A M J J A S O N D

Male/Female: *Summer*: Bright brown and speckled on head, back and breast; black tail; white belly; long bill is dark brown; feet and legs black. *Winter*: Light grey head, neck and chest; white cheeks, white belly; tail black. In flight: White on underwing; white bar on top side of wing.

Voice: Call is *kip* in flight. Chattering during feeding.
Food: Crustaceans, molluscs, marine worms, insects.

Purple Sandpiper
Calidris maritima

Observation Calendar

J F M A M J J A S O N D

Male/Female: *Winter*: Overall soft grey with dark brown spots and rust; chest fades to pale belly; orange bill is slightly curved down which becomes black at end; dark eye with white eye-ring; legs and feet yellow / orange. In flight: White wing band; white rump on sides; dark underparts.

Voice: Call is a *twheeeet* and *twiiit*.
Food: Crustaceans, molluscs, insects, seeds and algae.

Spotted Sandpiper

Actitis macularia

Foot: Anisodactyl

Flying

Feeding

Observation Calendar

J F M A M J J A S O N D

Male/Female: *Summer*: Grey-brown on head, back and wings; white eyebrow and black line running from beak to back of neck; long orange bill; white chin, chest and belly with distinct charcoal spots; yellow feet and legs; bobbing tail.
Winter: White underparts — no spots. In flight: Quick stiff wingbeats, slightly arched back.

Voice: Quiet bird but makes a *peeetaawet* call during courtship and a whistle that is repeated when alarmed.
Food: Insects, worms, crustaceans, fish, flies and beetles.
Nest/Eggs: Shallow depression on ground lined with grasses and mosses. 4 eggs.

Egg: Actual Size

White-rumped Sandpiper

Calidris fuscicollis

Size Identification

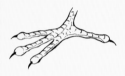

Foot: Anisodactyl

Flying

Feeding

Observation Calendar

J F M A M J J A S O N D

Male/Female: *Spring and Summer*: Light grey and rufous brown speckled with darker browns on head, back and wings; chest speckled lighter buff fading to white on belly; bill black with red underside; tail and wing tips dark brown and black; feet and legs black. *Winter*: Colours change to grey overall. In flight: White rump; white under wings.

Voice: Call is high-pitched *jeeeeeet* and *twitter*.
Food: Crustaceans, worms, snails, insects.

Greater Scaup

Aythya marila

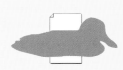

Foot: Tridactyl

Flying

Feeding

Observation Calendar
J F M A M J J A S O N D

Male: *Winter*: Dark green iridescent head neck and chest; white sides and belly; large flat grey bill; yellow eye; grey back with thin black banding; stubby black tail; black feet and legs. *Summer*: Sides and belly brown; head, neck and chest dull brown-black. In flight: Large white patches on inside of wings.
Female: Overall dark brown with white face patch. Head held lower than male. In flight: Large white patches on trailing edge of wings.

Voice: Male — repeated *waaahooo*. Female — growling *arrrrr*. Mostly quiet.
Food: Aquatic plants, crustaceans, molluscs, snails.
Nest/Eggs: Cup-shaped clump of grasses and aquatic plants on ground, lined with down. Often builds on islands. 8-12 eggs.

Black Scoter
Melanitta nigra

Size Identification

Foot: Tridactyl

Flying

Feeding

Observation Calendar

J F M A M J J A S O N D

Male: Overall black with long thin tail feathers; large yellow knob on top of black bill; feet and legs dark orange.
Female: Overall dark grey with lighter grey on cheeks.

Voice: Low whistle during courtship. Quiet.
Food: Aquatic plants, molluscs, mussels, limpets.

Surf Scoter

Melanitta perspicillata

Size Identification

Foot: Tridactyl

Flying

Feeding

Observation Calendar

J F M A M J J A S O N D

Male: Overall black with white patches on forehead and back of neck; yellow eye; distinctive large orange and red bill with black and white patches on sides.

Female: Overall dark brown with large black bill and vertical white patch behind it; top of head is slightly darker. In flight: Pale grey belly.

Did you know? Easy spotting on the Surf Scoter is to look for birds diving directly into the breaking surf hunting for molluscs or crustaceans.

Voice: Male — low whistle during courtship.
Food: Mussels, crustaceans, insects, aquatic plants.

White-winged Scoter

Melanitta fusca

Foot: Tridactyl

Flying

Feeding

Observation Calendar

J F M A M J J A S O N D

Male: Black overall with yellow eye and white tear-shaped mark around eye; bill is orange, yellow and white; orange feet and legs. In flight: White wing patch.
Female: Brown overall; white oval on face; white patches on wings.

Voice: Female — low whistle. Male — in courtship is similar to ring of bell.
Food: Clams, scallops, mussels.

Greater Shearwater

Puffinus gravis

Observation Calendar
J F M A M J J A S O N D

Male/Female: Black cap and bill; white chin, breast and belly; dark grey back with lighter grey markings; dark tail feathers; feet and legs black. In flight: Slight banding on tail feathers; underwing white outlined in dark grey.

Voice: Loud *squeeee* when aggressive. Mostly silent.
Food: Small fish, squid, crustaceans at water's surface.
Nest/Eggs: Colonies. Small amounts of grass at end of burrow on grassy slope. 1 egg.

Manx Shearwater
Puffinus puffinus

Size Identification

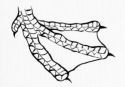

Foot: Tridactyl

Flying

Feeding

Observation Calendar
J F M A M J J A S O N D

Male/Female: Black upper body extending just below eye; pale grey breast blending around face and collar with black; white flank and belly; short rounded tail; feet and legs black. Wing underparts white with grey blending to black tips. In flight: Quick wingbeats with long glides.

Voice: Mostly quiet. Occasional coo or cluck when breeding.
Food: Small fish, crustaceans and squid at water's surface.

Sooty Shearwater

Puffinus griseus

Size Identification

Foot: Tridactyl

Flying

Feeding

Observation Calendar

J F M A M J J A S O N D

Male/Female: Overall dark grey, brown and sooty black with pale grey under wings; charcoal and black bill; legs and feet dark. In flight: Quick wingbeats with occasional gliding.

Voice: Variety of coos and clucks in courtship. Mostly silent.
Food: Small fish and squid at surface. Occasionally will dive for fish.

Common Snipe

Gallinago gallinago

Observation Calendar

J F M A M J J A S O N D

Male/Female: Very long narrow bill; with small head and large brown/black eye; buff eye ring; black and white bars on white belly; brown back striped with pale yellow; short yellow feet and legs; tail has rust band. In flight: Pointed wings; flies in back and forth motion with quick wingbeats.

Did you know? The Common Snipe uses its long bill to hunt in bog-like conditions where it can penetrate through the soft ground to catch prey below the surface.

Voice: Call is a *swheet swheet* with sharp *scaip* call when flushed.
Food: Larvae, crayfish, molluscs, insects, frogs and seeds.
Nest/Eggs: Hollow in marsh area, concealed with grass, leaves, twigs and moss. 4 eggs.

Sora

Porzana carolina

Size Identification

Foot: Anisodactyl

Flying

Feeding

Observation Calendar

J F M A M J J A S O N D

Male/Female: Chicken-like; grey above eye runs down to chin, breast and belly; black mask behind thick yellow bill; upper parts chestnut brown with white and dark brown bars; legs and feet yellow; buff rump.

Did you know? The Sora, like other rails, prefers to migrate at night.

Voice: Call is musical *kuur weeee* which is repeated and descends.
Food: Aquatic insects and seeds.
Nest/Eggs: Built in open marsh, attached to reeds, using leaves and grass. 6-15 eggs.

Egg: Actual Size

Arctic Tern
Sterna paradisaea

Size Identification

Size Identification

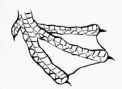

Foot: Tridactyl

Flying

Feeding

Observation Calendar
J F M A M J J A S O N D

Male/Female: Black head with long sharp red bill; overall grey; exceptionally long thin tail; red feet and legs are very short; In flight: White rump and lower back.

Did you know? Terns have the ability to hover over the surface of the water when hunting for prey.

Voice: Loud high-pitched *kee ar* or *kip-kip-kip-kee-ar.*
Food: Small fish.
Nest/Eggs: On ground, lined with grasses and shells, on rocky ledge or beach, often in colonies, isolated from human habitation. 2 eggs.

Egg: Actual Size

Black Tern

Childonias niger

Foot: Tridactyl

Flying

Feeding

Observation Calendar

J F M A M J J A S O N D

Male/Female: *Summer*: Black head, bili, chest and belly; white rump; feet and legs black; wings and tail charcoal. *Winter*: Wings and back charcoal; head white with black on top; white chest and underparts.

Did you know? This is one very fast bird. The Black Tern catches insects in flight.

Voice: Call is short *kirc* of *keeeel*.
Food: Insects.
Nest: Colonies. Loosely built pile of aquatic plants and grasses on water's edge or floating on water. 3 eggs.

Egg: Actual Size

89

Common Tern

Sterna hirundo

Size Identification

Size Identification

Foot: Tridactyl

Flying

Feeding

Observation Calendar

J F M A M J J A S O N D

Male/Female: *Summer*: Soft grey overall with black-cap; white cheeks; long thin red bill with black tip; short, red feet and legs; wings and tail feathers grey, exceptionally long; white underside to tail.
Winter: Black cap receeds leaving white face; black bar on wing; charcoal on tail. In flight: Charcoal on wing tips; grey overall; quick wingbeats.

Voice: Short *kip* repeated and louder *keeeear.*
Food: Small fish.
Nest/Eggs: Colonies. On ground, cup of grasses on sandy or pebbled areas. Most often on islands. 2-3 eggs.

Egg: Actual Size

Ruddy Turnstone

Arenaria interpres

Observation Calendar

J F M A M J J A S O N D

Male/Female: *Winter*: Speckled brown back, head and wings; white belly, brown bib and white patch on either side; feet and legs dark orange. *Summer*: Overall upperparts brown and black; brown and black bill with white patch just behind bill; black bib with white patch; short black tail. In flight: White bands on wings and back.

Did you know? The Ruddy Turnstone got its name because of its feeding habits. The bird wanders down the feeding area turning over stones.

Voice: Call is *tuc e tuc*.
Food: Insects, molluscs, crustaceans, marine worms.

American Wigeon

Anas americana

Size Identification

Foot: Tridactyl

Flying

Feeding

Observation Calendar
J F M A M J J A S O N D

Male: White patch running up forehead from bill; green around eye broadening at cheeks and descending on neck; brown changing to black on back and extremely pointed wings; pointed tail feathers are black, lines with white; bill white with black patches on top and on tip. In flight: Green on trailing edge of wing; white forewing and belly.
Female: Overall light brown with brighter colour running down sides. No green patch on eye.

Did you know? The American Wigeon is an opportunist: waiting for other diving ducks to come to the surface with their catch, they will attempt to steal the food.

Voice: Male — occasional distinctive whistle *wh-wh-whew.* Female quacks.
Food: Aquatic plants.
Nest/Eggs: Grasses lined with down, concealed under brush or tree, a distance from water. 9-12 eggs.

Egg: 90%

92

Willet

Catoptrophorus semipalmatus

Observation Calendar

J F M A M J J A S O N D

Male/Female: Brownish grey and white speckled; white at lower belly and rump; bill is long, heavy greyish yellow; feet and legs grey; black tip on wings.
In flight: Distinctive bold white wing band on black tipped wings.

Voice: Call is ring-like similar to name *pill will willet* with quieter call *kip* repeated 3-6 times.
Food: Insects, crustaceans, molluscs, grasses and seeds.
Nest/Eggs: On open ground, lined with grasses or bits of shell, a distance from water. 4 eggs.

Greater Yellowlegs
Tringa melanoleuca

Size Identification

Foot: Anisodactyl

Flying

Feeding

Observation Calendar

J F M A M J J A S O N D

Male/Female: Speckled grey and white overall; long bright yellow legs and feet; long straight black bill; short tail feathers with black banding; white belly.

Voice: Call is whistled musical *whew* repeated and descending.
Food: Fish, snails, insects, plants.
Nest/Eggs: Hollow on ground in damp area. 4 eggs.

Egg: Actual Size

Lesser Yellowlegs

Tringa flavipes

Observation Calendar

J F M A M J J A S O N D

Male/Female: Long black bill; dark upperparts speckled white; white belly; wings and tail feathers banded black; long yellow legs and feet.

Voice: Call is *tu* repeated.

Food: Insects, worms, snails, berries, small fish.